I0845613

Touching the Light:
The Remarkable Life of Helen Keller

Helen Keller was born on June 27, 1880, in Tuscumbia, Alabama. Her parents, Arthur Keller and Kate Adams, were both descended from prominent New England families, and her father was a respected newspaper editor and captain in the Confederate army during the Civil War.

However, tragedy struck when Helen was just 19 months old. She contracted an illness, which was most likely scarlet fever or meningitis, that left her deaf and blind. Her parents were devastated, and for the first few years of her life, Helen was completely cut off from the world around her. She became increasingly frustrated and isolated, and her parents were at a loss as to how to help her.

In desperation, they turned to Alexander Graham Bell, who had recently invented the telephone and was interested in helping deaf and blind children. Bell put them in touch with the Perkins Institute for the Blind in Boston, which recommended a young teacher named Anne Sullivan.

Anne Sullivan arrived in Tuscumbia in 1887, and it was immediately apparent that she had her work cut out for her.

Helen was a headstrong child who had never learned any formal communication skills and had little understanding of the world around her. But Anne was patient and persistent, and eventually, she made a breakthrough.

One day, while they were at the water pump, Anne spelled the word "water" into Helen's hand. Suddenly, everything clicked into place for Helen. She realized that everything had a name, and that those names could be communicated through finger spelling. Over the next few weeks and months, Anne taught Helen hundreds of words, and helped her develop a language of her own.

It wasn't easy, and there were many setbacks along the way. Helen was often frustrated and angry, and Anne had to be firm and patient in order to break through her defenses. But slowly but surely, Helen began to blossom. She became more curious and engaged with the world around her, and her parents were amazed at the transformation they saw in her.

In 1888, Anne and Helen moved to Boston, where Helen enrolled in the Perkins Institute. It was a challenging environment, as she was the only deaf and blind student there. But Anne was by her side every step of the way, and Helen soon proved herself to be a brilliant student.

She learned to read and write in Braille, and soon became fluent in English, French, German, and Latin.

Education and Advocacy

After her time at the Perkins Institute, Helen Keller continued her education at Radcliffe College. Despite her deafness and blindness, she proved to be an exceptional student, earning high scores in a wide range of subjects.

Helen's time at Radcliffe was not without its challenges, however. She often struggled to keep up with her classmates, who could take notes and read books more easily than she could. But she persevered, and her determination and hard work paid off when she graduated cum laude in 1904, becoming the first deaf and blind person to earn a Bachelor of Arts degree.

After graduation, Helen dedicated herself to advocacy work on behalf of people with disabilities. She became a well-known speaker and writer, using her own experiences to shed light on the challenges facing the deaf and blind community. She also worked tirelessly to improve the educational opportunities available to people with disabilities, believing that education was the key to unlocking their full potential.

In 1924, Helen joined the American Foundation for the Blind, serving as a member of the board of trustees for over 40 years. Through the foundation, she worked to raise awareness about the needs of the blind and deaf community, and lobbied for improved access to education and employment opportunities.

Helen also worked with the American Civil Liberties Union (ACLU), using her platform to advocate for the rights of all Americans, regardless of their disability.

Throughout her life, Helen Keller remained an advocate for the underrepresented and marginalized. She recognized that her own success was due, in large part, to the opportunities that had been afforded to her, and she was determined to fight for those same opportunities for others.

Writing Career

Helen Keller's writing career is a testament to her incredible perseverance and talent. Despite her disabilities, she became a prolific writer, penning several books that are still celebrated today.

Her most famous work, "The Story of My Life," is an autobiography that details her early years, including her illness and subsequent loss of sight and hearing, as well as her education with Anne Sullivan. The book was an instant success, and has since become a classic of American literature. It has been translated into over 50 languages and has sold millions of copies worldwide.

In addition to "The Story of My Life," Helen Keller also wrote several other books, including "The World I Live In" and "Out of the Dark." These books provide insight into her thoughts and experiences as a person living with disabilities, and are still widely read and studied today.

Helen's writing career was not without its challenges, however. She often struggled to find the right words to express her ideas, and relied heavily on the assistance of her secretary, Polly Thompson, who helped her with everything from typing to editing.

Despite these challenges, Helen's writing was characterized by a unique voice and a deep sense of empathy. She was able to communicate the experience of living with disabilities in a way that was both insightful and moving, and her writing continues to inspire readers today.

Helen's writing also had a profound impact on the way that people with disabilities were perceived in society. Through her books and speeches, she challenged the notion that people with disabilities were somehow less capable or deserving than their able-bodied counterparts. She argued that with the right opportunities and support, anyone could achieve great things.

Political Activism

Helen Keller's activism extended far beyond her advocacy for people with disabilities. She was a passionate advocate for social justice and used her platform to promote causes that she believed would create a fairer and more equal society.

One of Helen's most significant contributions to the political landscape was her support of women's suffrage. She recognized that women's right to vote was a fundamental issue of fairness and equality, and worked tirelessly to promote this cause. She spoke at rallies and demonstrations across the country, and used her writing to raise awareness about the importance of women's suffrage.

Helen's activism also extended to workers' rights. She was a strong supporter of labor unions and believed that workers should be able to organize and advocate for fair wages and better working conditions. She was involved with the Industrial Workers of the World (IWW), a radical union that fought for workers' rights in the early 20th century.

Helen's political views were strongly influenced by her belief in pacifism. She was a vocal opponent of war and believed that violence only led to more violence. During World War I, she was a leading voice in the anti-war movement, and worked to promote peace and understanding between nations.

Helen's political activism also led her to become involved with the Socialist Party of America. She saw socialism as a way to create a more just and equitable society, where everyone had access to the basic necessities of life, such as food, shelter, and healthcare. She believed that the government had a responsibility to provide these things to its citizens, and worked to promote these ideas through her writing and speeches.

Despite her radical views, Helen was never afraid to speak out for what she believed in. She was a fierce advocate for justice and equality, and used her platform to promote causes that were often unpopular at the time. Her courage and conviction inspired countless others to join the fight for social justice, and her legacy continues to inspire activists today.

Travel and Lecturing

Helen Keller's tireless advocacy work took her all around the world, where she inspired countless people with her message of hope and resilience. Her travels were not only an opportunity to promote her message, but also a chance to learn about different cultures and ways of life.

Helen's first trip abroad (along with Anne and Polly) was to Scotland, Ireland, and England in 1930, where she spoke to large audiences about the importance of education and social justice for people with disabilities.

Helen's travels continued throughout her life, and she visited countries such as Japan, India, and Egypt, where she met with political leaders, educators, and other activists. She used these opportunities to raise awareness about the challenges faced by people with disabilities in these countries, and to promote the establishment of schools and other services for people with disabilities.

In Japan, Helen was particularly moved by the plight of blind children, who had no access to education or other services. She worked tirelessly to establish a school for the blind in Tokyo, and her efforts paid off when the Helen Keller School for the Blind was opened in 1948. This school remains a testament to Helen's dedication to improving the lives of people with disabilities around the world.

Helen's travels provided her with the opportunity to share her message with audiences around the world. She was a sought-after lecturer, and spoke to audiences in venues ranging from small town halls to large auditoriums. Her speeches were always inspiring, and she encouraged her audiences to never give up hope, no matter how difficult their circumstances may be.

Later Years and Legacy

In her later years, Helen was accompanied by her lifelong companion, Polly Thompson. Polly was a dedicated caregiver and friend, and she remained by Helen's side until her death in 1960. Despite her own declining health, Helen remained active in her advocacy work, and continued to travel and speak to audiences around the world. Helen Keller passed away on June 1, 1968, at her home in Westport, Connecticut. She was 87 years old.

Helen's legacy as a symbol of hope and inspiration to people with disabilities around the world remains as strong as ever. She proved that even in the face of great adversity, it is possible to overcome obstacles and achieve great things.

Helen's advocacy work laid the groundwork for the disability rights movement that would emerge in the latter half of the 20th century. Her tireless efforts to promote the rights of people with disabilities helped to pave the way for the passage of the Americans with Disabilities Act, which was signed into law in 1990.

Today, Helen Keller remains an iconic figure, revered for her strength, resilience, and unwavering commitment to social justice. Her life and legacy serve as an inspiration to people around the world, and her message of hope and perseverance continues to resonate with people of all ages and backgrounds.

The best and most
beautiful things in
the world cannot be
seen or even touched
– they must be felt
with the heart.

Be of good cheer...
No effort that we make
to attain something
beautiful is ever
lost. Sometime,
somewhere, somehow
we shall find that
which we seek. We
shall speak, yes, and
sing, too, as God
intended we should
speak and sing.

Your success and
happiness lie in you.
External conditions
are the accidents of
life, its outer
trappings.

I grow more and more
suspicious of the
political powers
that take men away
from their work and
set them shooting
one another.

Literature is my Utopia. Here I am not disenfranchised. No barrier of the senses shuts me out from the sweet, gracious discourse of my book friends. They talk to me without embarrassment or awkwardness. The things I have learned and the things I have been taught seem of ridiculously little importance compared with their "large loves and heavenly charities."

Be happy,
talk happiness.
Happiness calls out
responsive gladness
in others. There is
enough sadness in the
world without yours.

When one comes to
think of it, there
are no such things as
divine, immutable, or
inalienable rights.
Rights are things we
get when we are strong
enough to make good
our claim on them.

Joy is a spiritual
element that gives
vicissitudes unity
and significance.

The one I felt and still feel most is
lack of time. I used to have time to
think, to reflect, my mind and I. We
would sit together of an evening
and listen to the inner melodies of
the spirit, which one hears only in
leisure moments when the words of
some loved poet touch a deep, sweet
chord in the soul that until then
had been silent. But in college
there is no time to commune with
one's thoughts. One goes to college
to learn, it seems, not to think.
When one enters the portals of
learning, one leaves the dearest
pleasures--solitude, books and
imagination--outside with the
whispering pines. I suppose I ought
to find some comfort in the thought
that I am laying up treasures for
future enjoyment, but I am
improvident enough to prefer
present joy to hoarding riches
against a rainy day.

When I recollect the
treasure of friendship
that has been bestowed
upon me I withdraw all
charges against life.
If much has been denied
me, much, very much has
been given. So long as
the memory of certain
beloved friends lives
in my heart I shall say
that life is good.

Who shall dare let his
incapacity for hope or
goodness cast a shadow
upon the courage of
those who bear their
burdens as if they
were privileges?

The few own the many
because they possess the
means of livelihood of all
... The country is governed
for the richest, for the
corporations, the bankers,
the land speculators, and
for the exploiters of labor.
The majority of mankind are
working people. So long as
their fair demands - the
ownership and control of
their livelihoods - are set
at naught, we can have
neither men's rights
nor women's rights.
The majority of mankind is
ground down by industrial
oppression in order that
the small remnant may live
in ease.

We betray ourselves
into smallness when
we think the little
choices of each day
are trivial.

We, the people, are not
free. Our democracy is
but a name. We vote?
What does that mean?
It means we choose
between Tweedledee
and Tweedledum.
We elect expensive
masters to do our work
for us, and then blame
them because they
work for themselves
and for their class.

We need limitations and temptations to open our inner selves, dispel our ignorance, tear off disguises, throw down old idols, and destroy false standards. Only by such rude awakenings can we be led to dwell in a place where we are less cramped, less hindered by the ever-insistent External. Only then do we discover a new capacity and appreciation of goodness and beauty and truth.

The mystery of
language was
revealed to me. I knew
then that 'W-A-T-E-R'
meant the wonderful
cool something that
was flowing over my
hand. That living
word awakened my
soul, gave it light,
joy, set it free.

We bereaved are not
alone. We belong to
the largest company
in all the world--
the company of those
who have known
suffering.

Character cannot be
developed in ease and
quiet. Only through
experience of trial
and suffering can the
soul be strengthened,
ambition inspired,
and success achieved.

What is the use
of such terrible
diligence as many
tire themselves out
with, if they always
postpone their
exchange of smiles
with Beauty and Joy
to cling to irksome
duties and relations?

If we do not like our
work, and do not try
to get happiness out
of it, we are a menace
to our profession as
well as to ourselves.

What do I consider a
teacher should be?
One who breathes
life into knowledge
so that it takes new
form in progress
and civilization.

I have walked with
people whose eyes are
full of light but who see
nothing in sea or sky,
nothing in city streets,
nothing in books.
It were far better to sail
forever in the night of
blindness with sense,
and feeling, and mind,
than to be content with
the mere act of seeing.
The only lightless dark
is the night of darkness
in ignorance and
insensibility.

To know the history of philosophy is to know that the highest thinkers of the ages, the seers of the tribes and the nations, have been optimists. The growth of philosophy is the story of man's spiritual life.

We can drift along
with general opinion
and tradition, or we
can throw ourselves
upon the guidance of
the soul within and
steer courageously
toward truth... We
have a choice in
every event and every
limitation and....to
choose is to create.

The world is sown with
good; but unless I turn
my glad thoughts into
practical living and
till my own field,
I cannot reap a kernel
of the good. The desire
and will to work is
optimism itself.

Although the world
is full of suffering,
it is full also of the
overcoming of it.
My optimism, then, does
not rest on the absence of
evil, but on a glad belief
in the preponderance of
good and a willing effort
always to cooperate with
the good, that it may
prevail.

One can never
consent to creep
when one feels an
impulse to soar.

Use your eyes as if
tomorrow you would be
stricken blind. Hear the
music of voices, the song
of birds, the mighty
strains of an orchestra as
if you would be stricken
deaf tomorrow . . . Smell
the perfume of flowers,
taste with relish each
morsel as if tomorrow you
could never smell and
taste again. Glory in all
the facts of pleasure and
beauty which the world
reveals to you.

The marvelous
richness of human
experience would
lose something of
rewarding joy if there
were no limitations to
overcome. The hilltop
hour would not be half
so wonderful if there
were no dark valleys
to traverse.

The woman who works
for a dollar a day
has as much right
as any other human
being to say what
the conditions of
her work should be.

I believe that God
is in me as the sun
is in the colour and
fragrance of a
flower – the Light
in my darkness, the
Voice in my silence.

Every optimist moves along with progress and hastens it, while every pessimist would keep the worlds at a standstill. The consequence of pessimism in the life of a nation is the same as in the life of the individual. Pessimism kills the instinct that urges men to struggle against poverty, ignorance and crime, and dries up all the fountains of joy in the world.

For three things I
thank God every day of
my life: thanks that
he has vouchsafed me
knowledge of his
works; deep thanks
that he has set in my
darkness the lamp of
faith; deep, deepest
thanks that I have
another life to look
forward to--a life
joyous with light and
flowers and heavenly
song.

We could never
learn to be brave
and patient, if
there were only joy
in the world.

A simple, childlike
faith in a Divine
Friend solves all
the problems that
come to us by land
or sea.

One's life story
cannot be told with
complete veracity.
A true autobiography
would have to be
written in states of
mind, emotions,
heartbeats, smiles
and tears; not in
months and years, or
physical events. Life
is marked off on the
soul by feelings, not
by dates.....

When one door of
happiness closes,
another opens; but
often we look so long
at the closed door
that we do not see the
one which has been
opened for us.

The best educated
human being is the
one who understands
most about the life in
which he is placed.

People do not like
to think. If one
thinks, one must
reach conclusions.
Conclusions are not
always pleasant.

It is curious to observe
what different ideals of
happiness people cherish,
and in what singular
places they look for this
well-spring of their life.
Many look for it in the
hoarding of riches, some in
the pride of power, and
others in the achievements
of art and literature; a few
seek it in the exploration
of their own minds, or in
search for knowledge.

When indeed shall we learn
that we are all related one
to the other, that we are all
members of one body? Until
the spirit of love for our
fellow people, regardless of
race, color, or creed, shall
fill the world, making real
in our lives and our deeds
the actuality of human
brother- and sisterhood,
until the great mass of the
people shall be filled with
the sense of responsibility
for each other's welfare,
social justice can never be
attained.

I am only one,
But still I am one.
I cannot do
everything,
But still I can do
something;
And because I cannot
do everything,
I will not refuse to
do the something
that I can do.

Faith is the strength
by which a shattered
world shall emerge
into the light.

When we complain of having
to do the same thing over and
over, let us remember that
God does not send new trees,
strange flowers and
different grasses every year.
When the spring winds blow,
they blow in the same way. In
the same places the same dear
blossoms lift up the same
sweet faces, yet they never
weary us. When it rains, it
rains as it always has. Even
so would the same tasks
which fill our daily lives
put on new meanings if we
wrought them in the spirit
of renewal from within--a
spirit of growth and beauty.

Strike against war, for
without you no battles
can be fought. Strike
against manufacturing
shrapnel and gas bombs
and all other tools of
murder. Strike against
preparedness that means
death and misery to
millions of human
beings. Be not dumb,
obedient slaves in an
army of destruction.
Be heroes in an army
of construction.

The highest result of
education is tolerance.
Long ago men fought and
died for their faith; but it
took ages to teach them the
other kind of courage, —
the courage to recognize
the faiths of their brethren
and their rights of
conscience. Tolerance is
the first principle of
community; it is the spirit
which conserves the best
that all men think.

Great poetry needs
no interpreter
other than a
responsive heart.

The civilization
of a state should be
measured by the
amount of suffering
it prevents and the
degree of happiness
it makes possible
for its citizens.

Education should
train the child to use
his brains, to make for
himself a place in the
world and maintain
his rights even when
it seems that society
would shove him into
the scrap-heap.

The infinite wonders
of the universe are
revealed to us in exact
measure as we are
capable of receiving
them. The keenness of
our vision depends not
on how much we can see,
but on how much we feel.

A smile goes a long
way, but you must
first start it on
its journey.

Everybody talks,
nobody listens. Good
listeners are as rare
as white crows.

If we spend the time
we waste in sighing
for the perfect golden
fruit in fulfilling
the conditions of its
growth, happiness
will come, must come.
It is guaranteed in
the very laws of the
universe. If it
involves some
chastening and
renunciation, well,
the fruit will be all
the sweeter for this
touch of holiness.....

Faith is a mockery if
it does not teach us
that we can build a
more complete and
beautiful world.

Smell is a potent
wizard that transports
you across thousand of
miles and all the years
you have lived.

The wise fools who sit
in the high places of
justice fail to see that
in revolutionary
times vital issues
are settled not by
statutes, decrees and
authorities, but in
spite of them.

One painful duty
fulfilled makes the
next plainer and
easier.

What we have once
enjoyed we can never
lose. All that we love
deeply becomes a part
of us.

For, after all, every one who
wishes to gain true knowledge
must climb the Hill Difficulty
alone, and since there is no
royal road to the summit, I
must zigzag it in my own way.
I slip back many times, I fall,
I stand still, I run against the
edge of hidden obstacles,
I lose my temper and find it
again and keep it better,
I trudge on, I gain a little,
I feel encouraged, I get more
eager and climb higher and
begin to see the widening
horizon. Every struggle is a
victory. One more effort and I
reach the luminous cloud, the
blue depths of the sky, the
uplands of my desire.

Instead of comparing our lot with that of those who are more fortunate than we are, we should compare it with the lot of the great majority of our fellow men. It then appears that we are among the privileged.

...our enjoyment of
the great works of
literature depends
more upon the depth
of our sympathy
than upon our
understanding.

Doubt and mistrust
are the mere panic of
timid imagination,
which the steadfast
heart will conquer,
and the large mind
transcend.

Certainly I believe that God
gave us life for happiness,
not misery. Humanity, I am
sure, will never be made lazy
or indifferent by an excess
of happiness. Many persons
have a wrong idea of what
constitutes true happiness.
It is not attained through
self-gratification but
through fidelity to a worthy
purpose. Happiness should be
a means of accomplishment,
like health, not an end in
itself.

Security is mostly a superstition. It does not exist in nature, nor do the children of men as a whole experience it. Avoiding danger is no safer in the long run than outright exposure. Life is either a daring adventure, or nothing.

It is a mistake always
to contemplate the
good and ignore the
evil, because by
making people
neglectful it lets in
disaster. There is a
dangerous optimism
of ignorance and
indifference.

Even more amazing
than the wonders of
Nature are the
powers of the
spirit.

The danger of having
the Constitution
twisted and
misconstrued to
support vested
interests and
prejudices must be
guarded against if
American democracy
is to maintain a
progressive
character.

Deep, solemn optimism, it
seems to me, should spring
from this firm belief in
the presence of God in the
individual; not a remote,
unapproachable governor
of the universe, but a God
who is very near every one
of us, who is present not
only in earth, sea and sky,
but also in every pure and
noble impulse of our
hearts.

Happiness is like the
mountain summit. It
is sometimes hidden
by clouds, but we
know it is there.

There is no better
way to thank God for
your sight than by
giving a helping
hand to someone in
the dark.

It is hard to
interest those who
have everything
in those who have
nothing.

I regard
philanthropy as a
tragic apology for
wrong conditions
under which human
beings live.

Four things to learn
in life: To think
clearly without hurry
or confusion; To love
everybody sincerely;
To act in everything
with the highest
motives; To trust God
unhesitatingly.

A person who is
severely impaired
never knows his
hidden sources of
strength until he is
treated like a normal
human being and
encouraged to shape
his own life.

Face your deficiencies
and acknowledge them;
but do not let them
master you. Let them
teach you patience,
sweetness, insight.
True education
combines intellect,
beauty, goodness, and
the greatest of these is
goodness. When we do
the best that we can,
we never know what
miracle is wrought in
our life, or in the life
of another.

Each day comes to me
with both hands full
of possibilities.

I believe it is a sacred duty to
encourage ourselves and others;
to hold the tongue from any
unhappy word against God's
world, because no man has any
right to complain of a universe
which God made good, and which
thousands of men have striven to
keep good. I believe we should so
act that we may draw nearer and
more near the age when no man
shall live at his ease while
another suffers. These are the
articles of my faith, and there is
yet another on which all depends
— to bear this faith above every
tempest which overfloods it, and
to make it a principal in
disaster and through affliction.
Optimism is the harmony between
man's spirit and the spirit of God
pronouncing His works good.

It gives me a deep
comforting sense
that Things seen are
temporal and things
unseen are eternal.

I am just as deaf as I am
blind. The problems of
deafness are deeper and
more complex, if not
more important, than the
problems of blindness.
Deafness is a much worse
misfortune. For it means
the loss of the most
vital stimulus — the
sound of the voice that
brings language, sets
thoughts astir and keeps
us in the intellectual
company of man.

The test of a
democracy is not the
magnificence of
buildings or the
speed of automobiles
or the efficiency of
air transportation,
but rather the care
given to the welfare
of all the people.

It is so pleasant to
learn about new
things. Every day I
find how little I
know, but I do not
feel discouraged
since God has given
me an eternity in
which to learn more.

There are times when I long
to sweep away half the things
I am expected to learn; for
the overtaxed mind cannot
enjoy the treasure it has
secured at the greatest cost.
... When one reads hurriedly
and nervously, having in
mind written tests and
examinations, one's brain
becomes encumbered with a
lot of bric-a-brac for which
there seems to be little use.
At the present time my mind
is so full of heterogeneous
matter that I almost despair
of ever being able to put it
in order.

A happy life consists
not in the absence,
but in the mastery
of hardships.

To keep our faces
toward change and
behave like free
spirits in the
presence of fate
is strength
undefeatable.

The best preparation
[for war] is the one
that disarms the
hostility of other
nations and makes
friends of them.

It is wonderful how
much time good people
spend fighting the
devil. If they would
only expend the same
amount of energy loving
their fellow men, the
devil would die in his
own tracks of ennui.

The bulk of the
world's knowledge
is an imaginary
construction.

What really counts
in life is the quiet
meeting of every
difficulty with the
determination to get
out of it all the
good there is.

I long to accomplish a
great and noble task;
but it is my chief duty
and joy to accomplish
humble tasks as though
they were great and
noble.... the world is
moved along, not only
by the mighty shoves of
its heroes, but also by
the aggregate of the
tiny pushes of each
honest worker.

It all comes to this:
the simplest way to be
happy is to do good.

Trying to write is
very much like
trying to put a
Chinese puzzle
together. We have a
pattern in mind
which we wish to
work out in words;
but the words will
not fit the spaces,
or, if they do, they
will not match the
design.

Once I knew the depth
where no hope was and
darkness lay on the
face of all things.
Then love came and
set my soul free.

No pessimist ever
discovered the
secret of the stars,
or sailed to an
uncharted land,
or opened a new
doorway for the
human spirit.

With every friend I
love who has been taken
into the brown bosom of
the earth a part of me
has been buried there;
but their contribution
to my being of
happiness, strength
and understanding
remains to sustain me
in an altered world.

That the sky is
brighter than the
earth means little
unless the earth
itself is appreciated
and enjoyed. Its
beauty loved gives
the right to aspire to
the radiance of the
sunrise and sunset.

I sometimes wonder if
the hand is not more
sensitive to the
beauties of sculpture
than the eye. I should
think the wonderful
rhythmical flow of
lines and curves could
be more subtly felt
than seen. Be this as it
may, I know that I can
feel the heart-throbs
of the ancient Greeks
in their marble gods
and goddesses.

I wonder what becomes
of lost opportunities?
Perhaps our guardian
angel gathers them up
as we drop them, and
will give them back to
us in the beautiful
sometime when we have
grown wiser, and
learned how to use
them rightly.

www.ingramcontent.com/pod-product-compliance
Lightning Source LLC
Chambersburg PA
CBHW012259240726
48656CB00007B/2449